MOUNTAINS

SEYMOUR SIMON

HOUGHTON MIFFLIN BOSTON • MORRIS PLAINS, NJ
California • Colorado • Georgia • Illinois • New Jersey • Texas

PHOTO AND ART CREDITS
Permission to use the following photographs is gratefully acknowledged:
page 4, Lewis Kemper/Denali National Park & Reserve, Alaska; pages 6, 7, 29, 31, Galen Rowell;
page 11, NASA; page 15, Alan G. Nelson/Dembinsky Photo Associates;
page 17, Willard Clay/Dembinsky Photo Associates;
page 19 (bottom), Adam Jones/Dembinsky Photo Associates;
page 25, Robert Mackinlay; page 32, from *The Art of Adventure,* Collins Publishers, 1989;
all other photographs by Seymour Simon.
Artwork on pages 13, 14, 16, and 18 by Ann Neumann,
Front cover photograph by Galen Rowell.
The text type is 18-point ITC Garamond Book.

Houghton Mifflin Edition, 2001

Printed in the U.S.A.

ISBN: 0-618-05988-1

23456789-B-06 05 04 03 02 01 00

To JOyce and ELizabeth

and their grandson

JOEL

Mountains are a dramatic reminder of ages past and ages to come. They seem to be solid and unchanging, but they are not everlasting. Mountains are born, grow tall over the years, change their shapes, and are finally worn down and disappear into the earth from which they came. These processes take millions of years, but a million years in the life of our planet is like a few days in the life of a person.

Mount McKinley, at over 20,000 feet, is the highest mountain in North America.

Mountains are tall, but just how tall does one have to be to be called a mountain? The Himalayan Mountains in central Asia have at least fourteen peaks over 26,000 feet. Mount Everest in the Himalayas (shown here) is the highest

mountain above sea level in the world, 29,028 feet. That's five and a half miles above sea level, taller than the world's twenty-six tallest skyscrapers stacked one atop another.

The Alps of Europe, the Andes of South America, and the Rockies of western North America each have dozens of peaks taller than 10,000 feet. Air temperature drops about three degrees Fahrenheit for every one thousand feet of altitude, so the peaks of many tall mountains, such as the Jungfrau in the Alps (above), are always cold and are covered by snow year round.

The Appalachians are a group of old, worn mountains 1,200 miles long in the eastern United States. Only a few Appalachian peaks are as high as 6,000 feet and many are much lower. This hill in New York's Catskill Mountains is less than 3,000 feet above sea level. In the Himalayas or the Alps, mountains like this would be called foothills. Whether to call something a mountain seems to depend upon who is looking at it and how high its surroundings are.

Most mountains are not solitary peaks but part of long chains or ranges. The Himalayas are over 1,500 miles long and link up with other mountain ranges to stretch hundreds of miles farther. The top half of this satellite photograph shows part of the Himalayan range, including Mount Everest. The melting snows of the Himalayas form rivers that drain down onto the plain of the Ganges River in India. Few people live in cold, high mountains, but the low-level Ganges plain is warm, heavily planted with crops, and thickly populated. The line between the white snows of the upper slopes and the green forests of the foothills marks the edges of the Himalayas.

Mountain ranges do not arise just anyplace. Most are formed when *plates*, giant pieces of the earth's crust, push and pull against each other. The United States, Canada, Mexico, and part of the North Atlantic Ocean are on the North American plate. The Rockies and the coast ranges of the western United States and Canada were formed where the North American plate pushed against the Pacific plate.

The Mid-Atlantic Ridge, a 10,000-mile-long underwater mountain chain that stretches the length of the Atlantic Ocean, was formed where the North American plate pulled away from the Eurasian plate and the African plate. The islands of Iceland and Surtsey are actually the tops of volcanic mountain peaks reaching above the surface of the ocean, which covers most of the Mid-Atlantic Ridge.

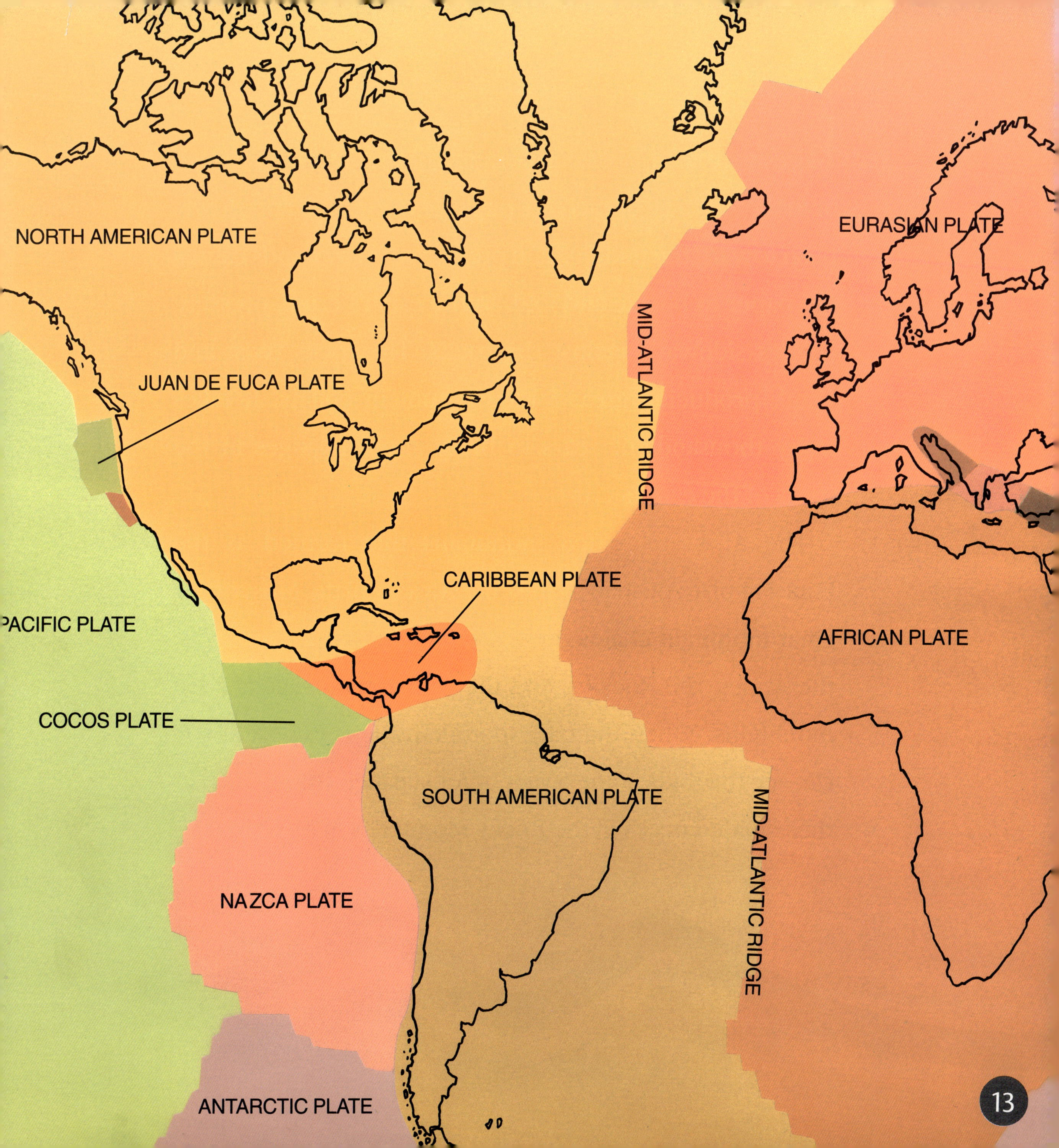
NORTH AMERICAN PLATE
EURASIAN PLATE
MID-ATLANTIC RIDGE
JUAN DE FUCA PLATE
CARIBBEAN PLATE
PACIFIC PLATE
AFRICAN PLATE
COCOS PLATE
SOUTH AMERICAN PLATE
MID-ATLANTIC RIDGE
NAZCA PLATE
ANTARCTIC PLATE

Rocks are hard, but with time and pressure they can bend or fold. Hold a large piece of paper at either end and slowly push toward the middle. The pressure of your hands causes the paper to buckle and fold. In the earth's crust, pressure pushes sideways against the rocks. The rocks twist and bend, producing great folded mountain chains. It takes many thousands of years to bring about changes in the rocks of the earth's crust.

The Alps are folded mountains that formed as the Eurasian plate pushed against the African plate. Most of the great mountain chains on earth, including the Himalayas, the Andes, the Rockies, and the Appalachians, are folded mountains. When the bare mountainside is exposed, you can see the folds in the layers of rock, called *strata*, such as these folded peaks in the Rocky Mountains in Montana.

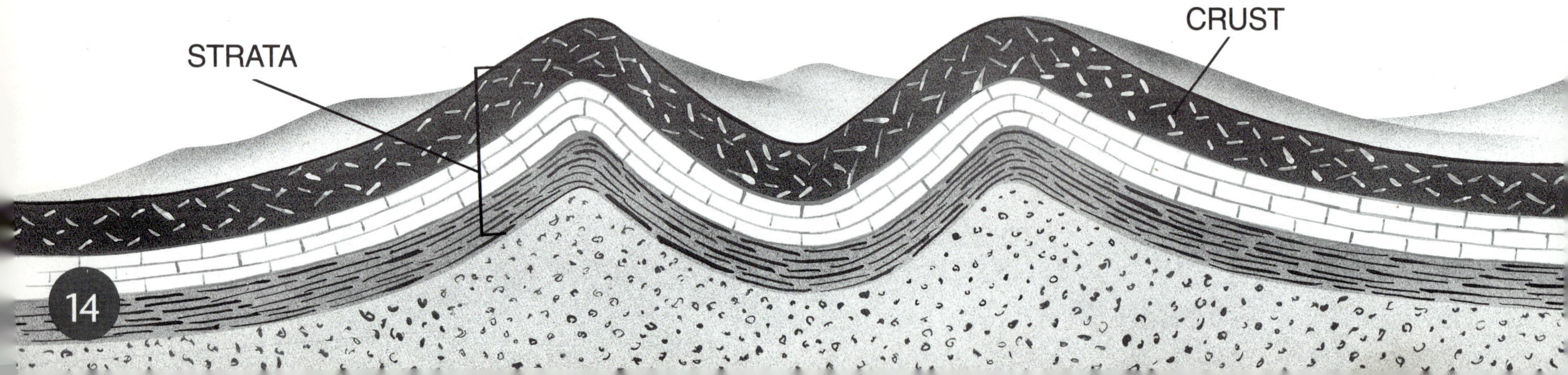

Another type of mountain is formed by the pulling apart or breaking of rocks. Faults are breaks in rock layers, and fault-block mountains form when one plate shifts or pulls away from another plate. Deep within the earth, hot currents of *magma*, molten rock, may well up and crack the weakened crust above. As the crust cracks, huge blocks of rock rise or fall, forming mountains. These mountains usually have a steep face on one side and a more gentle slope on the other side. The Sierra Nevada and the Grand Tetons of Wyoming (shown here) are examples of fault-block mountains.

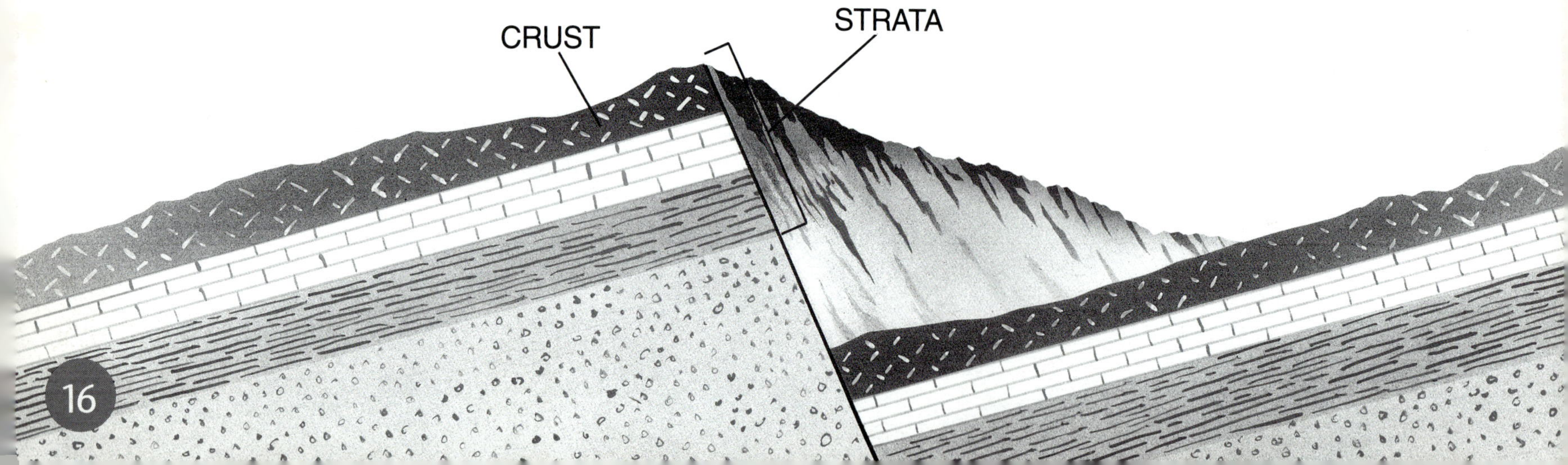

Still other mountains are formed by the eruption of volcanoes. During a volcanic eruption, magma squeezes up through cracks in the earth's crust and explodes out as lava and ash. When huge amounts of hardening lava and cinders pile up around the vent, or opening, they form a volcanic mountain, such as Mount Hood in Oregon (top right).

The Hawaiian Islands are the tops of volcanic mountains that rise 30,000 feet from the depths of the ocean, making them even taller than Everest if you measure from the ocean bottom. This aerial view of Hawaii (bottom right) shows some of its volcanic cinder cones.

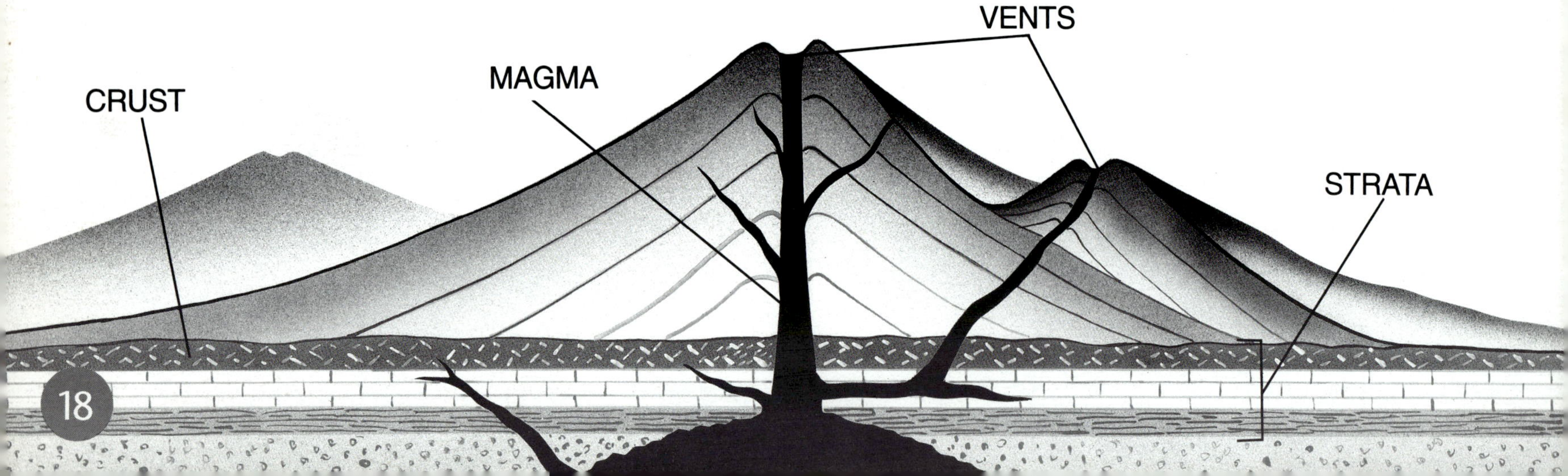

Dome mountains are formed by the same kind of molten rock that forms volcanic mountains. But dome mountains do not act or even look like volcanoes. They too result from a welling up of magma from deep within the earth through a crack in the earth's crust. However, in dome mountains, the magma does not come to the surface. Instead, the molten rock pushes the ground up into a round or dome-shaped bulge, and the magma gradually hardens into rock. When the softer rocks above are worn away, the great dome of underlying rock is revealed.

The Adirondacks of New York and the Black Hills of South Dakota are dome mountains. Yosemite's Half Dome (right) is a dome mountain that was cracked in half when sheets of granite fell off one side and were carried away by a glacier thousands of years ago.

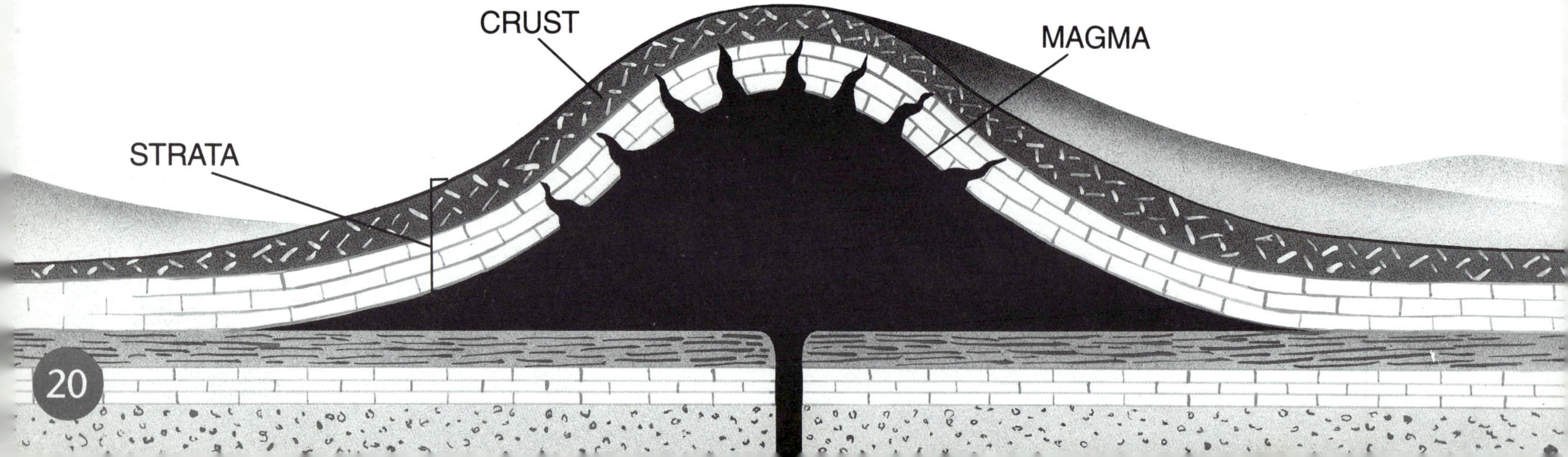

As soon as mountains rise, they begin to be worn down steadily and slowly by the forces of erosion: wind, rain, moving water, and ice, as well as temperature and chemical changes. Some kinds of rocks, such as limestone, dissolve in water, but most water erosion on mountains is caused by streams and rivers that plunge down the steep sides, lifting up rocks and pushing them along to rub and scrape against other rocks. In cold climates, slowly moving rivers of ice, called glaciers, also carve away at mountains.

Rocks expand daily in the heat of the sun and then contract again during the cold nights. These constant temperature changes begin to crack the rock. Water gets into the tiny cracks, freezes at night, expands, and opens the cracks wider. Finally, the rock breaks off from the mountain. Sometimes the wind blows sand, which wears away mountains to produce towers such as these in Zion National Park in Utah.

On steep mountain slopes, rocks tumble downhill pulled by gravity. Sometimes a rain shower or a small earthquake can send rocks roaring down the mountainside in a rock slide or rock avalanche. Rock glaciers, like those shown here on the slopes of Shivling Mountain in India, are rivers of small pieces of rock and soil frozen together that move slowly downhill like ice glaciers.

At the foot of a mountain, piles of broken boulders, smaller rocks, and soil often spread out in a fan-shaped pile called a *talus* slope. The material that makes up talus is called sliderock, and it continues to move downhill.

Mountains change shape slowly, but they have an immediate effect on weather and climate, especially on the amount of rainfall, the pattern of winds, and the movement of weather fronts. The reason for this is that mountains break up the flow of winds and force the air to move up or around. Air contains a certain amount of an invisible gas called water vapor. The cooler the air, the less water vapor it can hold. When air is forced to rise over a mountain, it gets colder and the water vapor condenses into tiny drops of water in clouds, mist, fog, and rain.

In the western United States, moisture-laden winds blow from the Pacific Ocean against the coastal mountain ranges of Washington, Oregon, and California. Clouds form and rain falls heavily on the rain forests of the western slopes. But on the eastern slopes of the mountains in these states, and in Wyoming, Montana, and Nevada, scarcely any rain falls at all. This is called the *rain shadow effect*. The driest deserts in America are separated from the wettest rain forests by only a few hundred miles.

Not all mountains are the same, but the change in life zones or habitats from the bottom to the top usually follows the same pattern. The lower slopes of mountains often have dense broadleaf forests of oak, poplar, or maple. On the middle slopes, it is colder and the kind of trees found changes to conifers, such as pine or spruce, which gradually become stunted and fewer in number. The upper limit of tree growth on a mountain is called the timberline, which ranges from about 11,000 feet in the southern Rockies to about 7,500 feet farther north. The higher slopes are dotted with clumps of low-growing alpine plants that can survive the harsh elements. In the fierce winds atop the peaks, nothing grows amid the ice- and snow-covered rocks.

On the lower slopes where many plants grow, there are also many kinds of animals. Higher up on the mountains, animals need to have special abilities to survive. Small animals eat the leaves and seeds of conifers. Surefooted and thickly furred grazers such as this mountain goat search for food even on the sheer slopes.

If you were to climb above 9,000 feet on a mountain, you would probably feel dizzy and short of breath. High up, the air contains less oxygen than at sea level. But there are people who live, work, and farm higher than 12,000 feet in the Himalayas and the Andes Mountains. These mountain people have developed more red blood cells, and this helps them utilize more oxygen from the air. Their bodies have adjusted to living in high places.

Many mountain people are herders. Their animals—usually yaks and buffalo in the Himalayas, llamas and alpacas in the Andes—provide them with milk, meat, and wool. Mountain soil is poor, and the steep land must be terraced if crops are to be grown. Terraces are small fields that have been cut into the steep sides of the mountains. Rocks are piled into walls at the end of each terrace to keep the soil from washing away. Barley is the chief crop in these Himalayan terraces. The rows of terraces make the mountainside look like a flight of steps for giants.

Not many people live on mountains, but mountains are important to all of us. Mountains create rain forests and deserts. Mountains store water on their snowy peaks and release it in rivers that make the valleys below green and fertile. Many farms and cities depend on mountain lakes for their drinking water, and the rivers are often harnessed to manufacture electricity. Mountains offer a chance for people to climb or ski or just take pleasure from some of the most spectacular scenery in the world.